High Energy Sales
THOUGHTS

101 Positive Sales Thoughts & Ideas

by CARL HENRY

© 2008 Carl Henry. All rights reserved. Printed and Bound in the United States of America. No part of this book my be reproduced or transmitted in any form or by any means, electronic or mechanical, including photocopying, recording, or by an information storage and retrieval system – except by a reviewer who may quote brief passages in a review to be printed in a magazine, newspaper, or on the Web – without permission in writing from the author. For information, please contact Henry Associates, 9430 Valley Road, Charlotte, NC 28270.

Cover and book design by Alex LaFasto

Although the author and publisher have made every effort to ensure the accuracy and completeness of information contained in this book, we assume no responsibility for errors, inaccuracies, omissions, or any inconsistency herein. Any slights of people, places, or organizations are unintentional.

First Printing 2008

ISBN 0-9657626-7-X

Nancy
Make selling fun!
Carl

introduction

Thoughts are funny things. They jump in and out of our minds, like raindrops, seeming to descend from nowhere only to vanish back into nothing.

But raindrops, like thoughts, hardly ever travel alone. And by looking at many of them, we can tell a great deal about the future. One or two, felt on a hot summer day, might mean nothing more than a sprinkling. If a few more show up, we might start to hope for a refreshing afternoon shower. But if enough of them arrive with speed and force, we know that a storm is coming.

Over time, storms grow into weather patterns that lead to enormous changes in our world. Paleontologists love to remind us that dinosaurs didn't live in our world – they lived in another one that just happened to be in the same place. In the millions of years since their time deserts have grown into jungles, rivers have chiseled canyons, and forests have sprung from dusty plains. All because raindrops came, again and again, until they were shaped into the world we see today.

Viewed in this light, raindrops deserve more of our respect. After all, they can turn a dusty, barren wasteland into a thriving mixture of fresh life just by showing up. Your thoughts are no different. Whatever you want to be – in sales or in life – is going to be dependent on what your thoughts shape you into. If your thoughts are lifeless, if they lack passion and excitement, then your career will be the same. But if they bring you energy and purpose, nourishing and encouraging you, then you can't help but find your way to the top.

Sales is a mental marathon. No single stride seems that important, but by putting some extra effort into every one of them we outperform our competition and become champions. Consider this book your daily warm-up run. In it, you'll find the attitudes and beliefs of top producers. Read through it once or twice a day until they become a part of your own mindset. You'll find that once you do, your success is as inevitable as a change in the weather.

Thought #1

Great salespeople have a burning desire to succeed. That's the edge that s e p a r a t e s them from the common employee.

Thought #2

It is great making sales! **BIG SALES,** little sales, they all feel fantastic. Selling validates our existence.

Thought #3

You don't apply for a multi-million dollar sales job. You  a multi-million dollar sales career.

Thought #4

It's easy to energize your sales career, just make a sale at a high margin.

Thought #5

There is a lot of **psychology** involved in selling. That's why most people can't do it.

Thought #6

Do things that create laaaaaaaaaaaasting success. Take action today and you'll get something positive tomorrow.

Thought #7

> Listen to your customers and they will tell you exactly how to sell them.

Thought #8

Don't worry about thinking

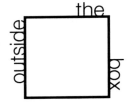

Think about what you can do today to make a sale.

Thought #9

You have to have

You can't prosper in this job unless you truly enjoy it.

Thought #10

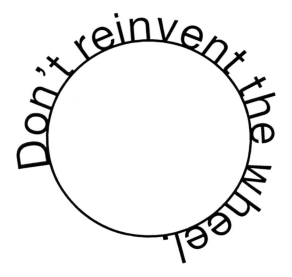

Learn how to sell correctly and then repeat that process.

Thought #11

First get the customer to trust you. And then, when they buy, deliver your solution with  passion!

Thought #12

It is more important to **understand** the principles of selling than the techniques of selling.

Thought #13

Set your goal to sell to the highest level of an organization, and then  the people that will eventually hold those positions.

Thought #14

Some customers are  **FORCEFUL** and strong-willed, others are steady and *relaxed.*

You need to learn how to sell to both styles.

Thought #15

If you are motivated by money and power 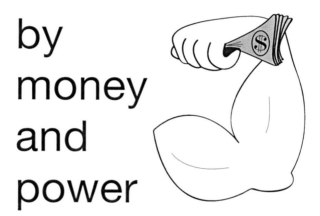 you possess the two most important values of a top sales producer.

Thought #16

Never be dependent on one source of sales income.

your customer base.

Thought #17

Great salespeople don't need to be motivated by their managers. They have personal *drive* and are determined to achieve their goals.

Thought #18

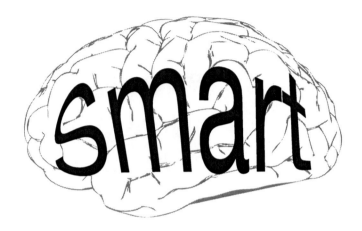

salespeople make it easy for people to do business with them.

Thought #19

If someone doesn't buy from you

remember they will buy from you

Thought #20

You can't  someone into buying your product or service.

Thought #21

Take a walk in the park and clear your mind. You won't just feel better, you'll make more sales.

Thought #22

Stay focused and remember it's all in the details.

Thought #23

Visit a trade show and you will see firsthand what is important to your customers.

Thought #24

Learn to speak in front of a group of people and your sales will **↑INCREASE** tremendously.

Thought #25

You must thoroughly understand everything about

Thought #26

People buy in spite of salespeople everyday.

Don't ever forget this.

Thought #27

You can't make someone buy from you. You must be in the position

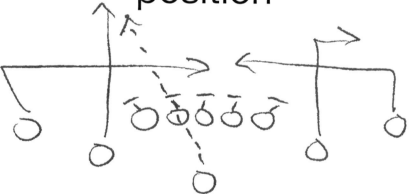

to help them when they want to buy.

Thought #28

People  the title of salesperson around too freely. Salespeople make most of their money from commissions.

Thought #29

Take the time to develop great sales habits early in your sales career.

Thought #30

Take a negotiating class and learn how to overcome your customer's tactics with your own counter tactics.

Thought #31

Remember most people don't like salespeople. Don't go into sales to please the **masses.**

Thought #32

Ask your customer intelligent questions and jot

them down on a clean sheet of paper.

Thought #33

I still believe that success is when opportunity and preparation meet. Your big

BREAK

may come today, be ready.

Thought #34

Very few people become successful working just 40 hours a week.

Name: Johnny Underpaid					
Mon	Tue	Wed	Thu	Fri	Total
8	8	8	8	8	40
8	8	8	8	8	40
8	8	8	8	8	40
8	8	8	8	8	40
8	8	8	8	8	40
8	8	8	8	8	40
8	8	8	8	8	40

Thought #35

Associate with top producers and other successful people. It will accelerate your

Thought #36

Doing a lot of things
is not the secret to success.

You must do the right things.

is not always a bad thing. It forces you to think.

Thought #38

They say you can become an expert in anything in five years. How many years will you wait before you learn how to sell?

Thought #39

When a customer buys from you they expect a great Return On *Investment*

Give it to them and they will keep buying.

Thought #40

People pay attention to what is **INTERESTING.** Is your presentation interesting? Are you interesting?

Thought #41

I have discovered that when a customer knows you appreciate their business, they give you more.

Thought #42

Do you have a sense of humor? Do you know how to make people laugh? Everyone likes to work with people that can make them

Thought #43

Pre-call sales

1. P
2. L
3. A
4. N
5. N
6. I
7. N
8. G

is very important. Don't get into the habit of selling by the seat-of-your pants.

Thought #44

Don't overestimate your own sales ability or underestimate your competitor's.

Thought #45

Money is just a by-product of doing what you 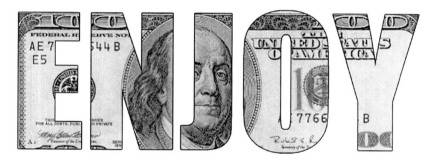 Concentrate on selling and the money will follow.

Thought #46

You should have some positive affirmation circling around in your head. My personal favorite is

Thought #47

Add some **body language** to your presentations. You'll seem more energetic and make more sales.

Thought #48

A determined person possesses a rare combination of **RUGGED** independence and esprit de corps.

Thought #49

Always give your customers

| GIVE > RECEIVE |

more than they expect to receive.

Thought #50

People won't buy the **WORST** product from a good salesperson, but will buy a **lesser** product from a great salesperson.

Thought #51

Persistence is sometimes the only thing we have, but it's all we need. If you refuse to ⊘QUIT, you will eventually succeed.

Thought #52

People usually believe what others say about you more than they believe what you say about yourself. Encourage others to sell you.

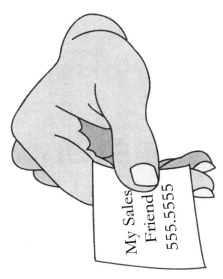

Thought #53

A customer once asked me,

Thought #54

Presenting in front of a group of decision makers is a great way to **multiply** your sales efforts. Look for opportunities to do this.

Thought #55

Want to learn how to sell? **Watch** other great salespeople in action. Observe what they do the same, not what they do differently.

Thought #56

If you fall down, stand up. Keep doing this until you stop falling down.

Thought #57

Stay away from negative people. I'm pretty positive about that statement.

Thought #58

If the customer tells you he or she wants to buy right now, and you suggest they think it over, then

reading this book and get another job.

Thought #59

You will get fewer price objections if you

concentrate

on your customer's needs first.

Thought #60

Top producers are confident and optimistic.

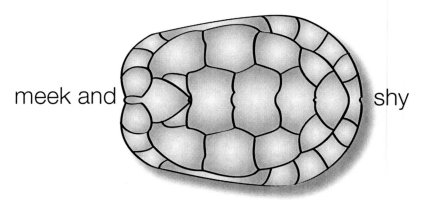

meek and shy

people are rarely great salespeople.

Thought #61

It is better to ask for the order **ONCE** at the right moment than six times at the wrong moment.

Thought #62

You must create systems to collect useful information about your customers and update it on a regular basis.

Thought #63

Prospecting will get customers into your sales funnel. Servicing will keep them buying. Do both.

Thought #64

Product knowledge is about 40% of the success formula,

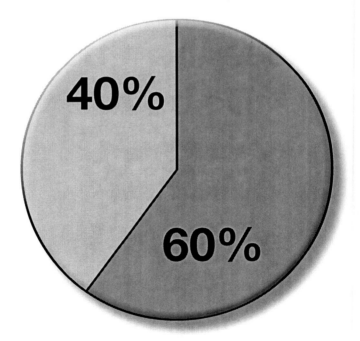

60% is sales skills and attitude.

Thought #65

Having empathy for your customer is important.

Sympathy

is dangerous and costly to your bottom line.

Thought #66

It's important to understand what your customer perceives as value, not what you perceive as

Thought #67

Big sales are great, but don't forget the little ones that keep that cash register (ringing) daily.

Thought #68

Make sure you show appreciation to your

INTERNAL

customers.

Thought #69

If it is true that you become what you think about most of the time, what do you think about most of the time?

I hope it's your sales career.

Thought #70

It's all about asking

the right ???

to the right 👫

at the right 🕐

Thought #71

If the customer asks you to cut the price, ask them why. Let them answer, build some value and then say no.

Thought #72

Spend your time finding out who has the power to make a decision before you

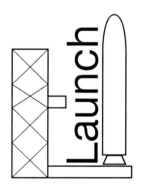

into a presentation.

Thought #73

You can't teach great timing to salespeople, but almost all top producers have it.

Thought #74

A great salesperson once told me he was successful because he thought about selling

all the time.

Thought #75

Selling is really not a normal job. The desire for money may get you into sales; the lifestyle will keep you in sales.

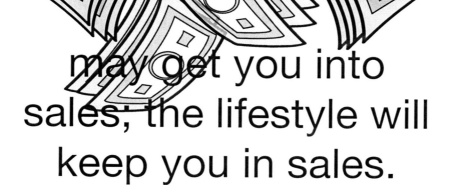

Thought #76

If you don't know where you are

You are here.

in the sales process, or where you're going, then you won't know what went wrong. And then you've got a big problem.

Thought #77

If you always have to be the **cheapest** to make the sale, you are not a professional salesperson.

Thought #78

Prepare written

???

in advance of meeting your customers.

Thought #79

You need to  your sales energy toward the completion of a goal without an external catalyst.

Thought #80

Learn to ask checking questions:

- ☑ Is this what you have in mind?
- ☑ How do you like this?

Thought #81

Hold eye contact and give your customer your full attention. They will

you by buying something.

Thought #82

Top salespeople

usually have a persuasive personality. Your job is to convince others to accept the best solution.

Thought #83

If you 🗣 you sell less, if you 👂 you sell more.

Thought #84

Do you have at least 50 sales books in your personal library?

Thought #85

Smart salespeople are problem solvers. The customer has a

you solve it. That's how you get paid.

Thought #86

customers become your second sales force.

Thought #87

Great salespeople have internal and external emotional control.

We are a lot stronger than most people think.

Thought #88

Multi-million dollar producers thnk differently. That is why they are multi-million dollar producers.

Thought #89

Everyone in your organization

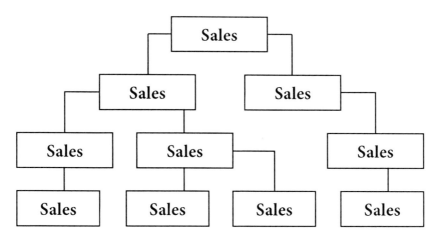

can help you sell. Be sure to treat them accordingly.

Thought #90

Take the time to learn about yourself.

Then you will understand the idiosyncrasies of your customers.

Thought #91

This profession is all about results. Don't **CONFUSE** activity with success. You are only fooling yourself.

Thought #92

Great salespeople have the ability to read between the lines in such things as body language, reticence, and emotions.

Thought #93

Too many sales are lost because salespeople don't stay  about their product or service.

Thought #94

Your personality either  attracts or repels others.

Do you have a pleasing personality?

Thought #95

Understanding the **complexity** of a sales situation is critical to your success.

Thought #96

When was the last time you sent a handwritten thank you note to a customer?

Thought #97

Your price is too HIGH

You will hear this from your first day in sales until you retire. Learn to overcome it!

Thought #98

Sales are like the ebb and flow of the tide.

When the tide is out remember it will return. Just keep working and it will return sooner.

Thought #99

Don't

forget

your mentors.
They were the
paradigm pioneers.
They showed you
that success was
obtainable.

Thought #100

great sales habits early in your sales career and you will eventually become an unconscious competent.

Thought #101

If this

is the only sales book you are reading you are in trouble. Start building your personal sales library immediately.

Carl Henry is a sales educator, keynote speaker and corporate consultant. During the course of his own successful career, he developed The MODERN Sales System, which he has been sharing with companies and associations around the world for many years.

A Certified Speaking Professional and a member of the National Speakers Association, Carl teaches essential sales skills with humor, insight and personal experience. Hundreds of companies throughout a diverse range of industries have used his highly-acclaimed seminars to educate and inspire their sales teams.

Carl's other books include *The MODERN Sales System*, *The PEOPLE Approach to Customer Service* and *15 Hot Tips that Will Supercharge Your Sales Career*.

He currently lives in Charlotte, North Carolina.

To order additional copies of this book, or find out about Carl's seminars contact him at:

Henry Associates
704-847-7390
9430 Valley Road
Charlotte, NC 28270
chenry@carlhenry.com
www.carlhenry.com

Printed in the United States
201731BV00003B/1-39/P